Women and Wine Coloring Book by Sally Rosenbaum
Copyright images belong to Sally Rosenbaum
Published November 16, 2017
All Rights Reserved
No image may be used for resale without the explicit consent of Sally Rosenbaum

Published by Ashby Press
Napa, California 94558

Women and Wine

Adult Coloring Book

Paintings
by
Sally Rosenbaum

Welcome

It's been great fun to draw the outlines of my paintings. I am including two of each image because it is fun to try to interpret the pictures in a variety of ways. Sometimes I like the foreground to be lightest with the background in a darker value and sometimes I reverse it and do what is known as back lighting where the figure is a little darker and the bright sun is behind the figure. It's fun to change it up.

I have included the paintings on the back cover so you may use them as reference material if you desire. On some paintings there are large expanses of table or clothing and I have found that it is most effective if you have lots of color changes within the surface.

Do not be afraid to color on top of other colors. When I paint I am often pushing warmer colors into cooler colors and vice versa.

The backgrounds on several paintings are very suggestive of abstract areas of foliage. I usually use this area to balance the painting with other colors I've used in the painting. Have fun with it.

Try using a limited number of colors and see what you can do by combining and layering the colors.

This painting is called My Afternoon. Here you have the wide expanse of the tablecloth. Try and put in lots of different colors to suggest the dappled use of sunlight and shadow. Feel free to make a lovely print on her dress. Patterns make it unique.

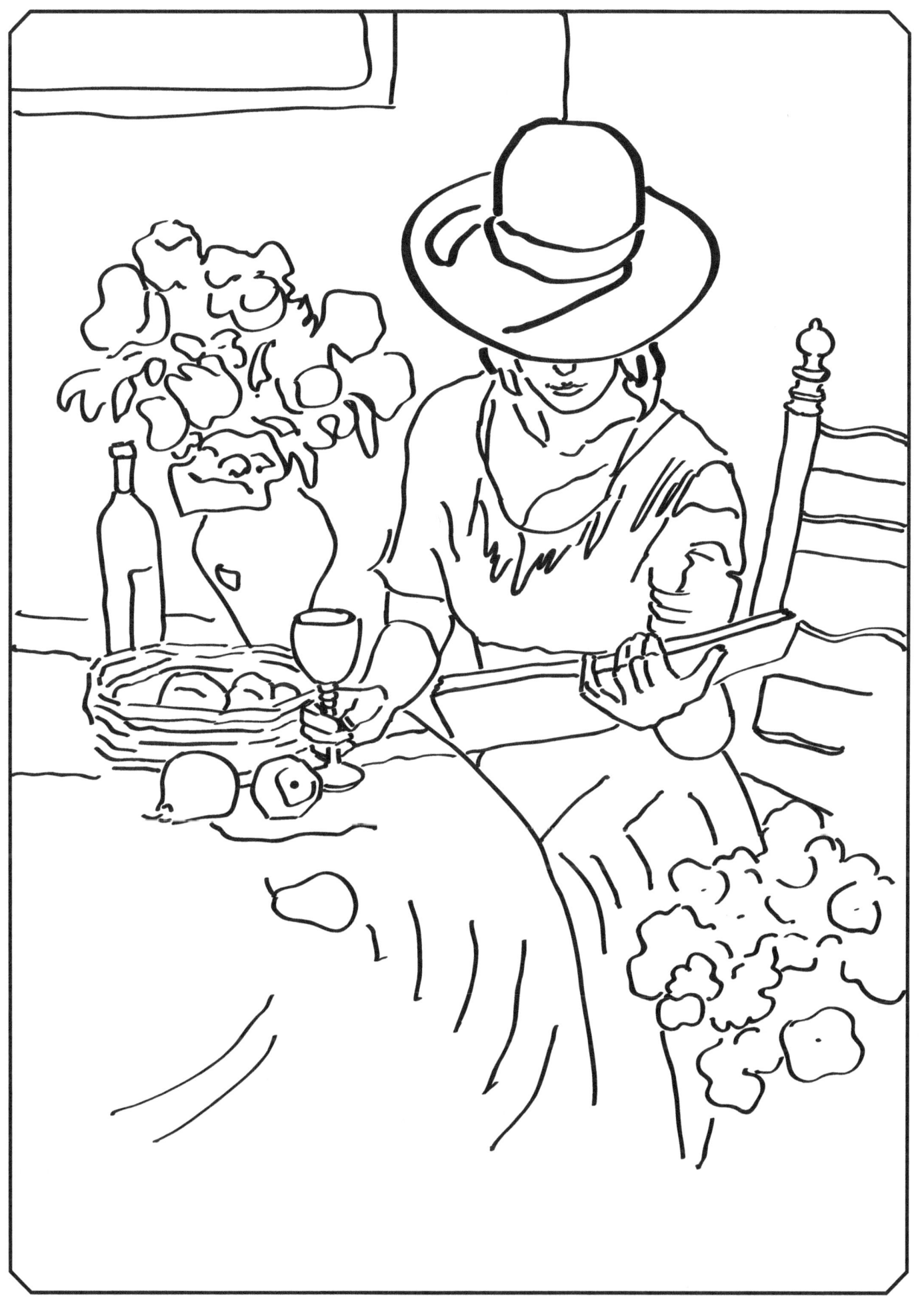

This painting is called Summer Moment and I have painted it myself in two very different styles. Have fun with the background.

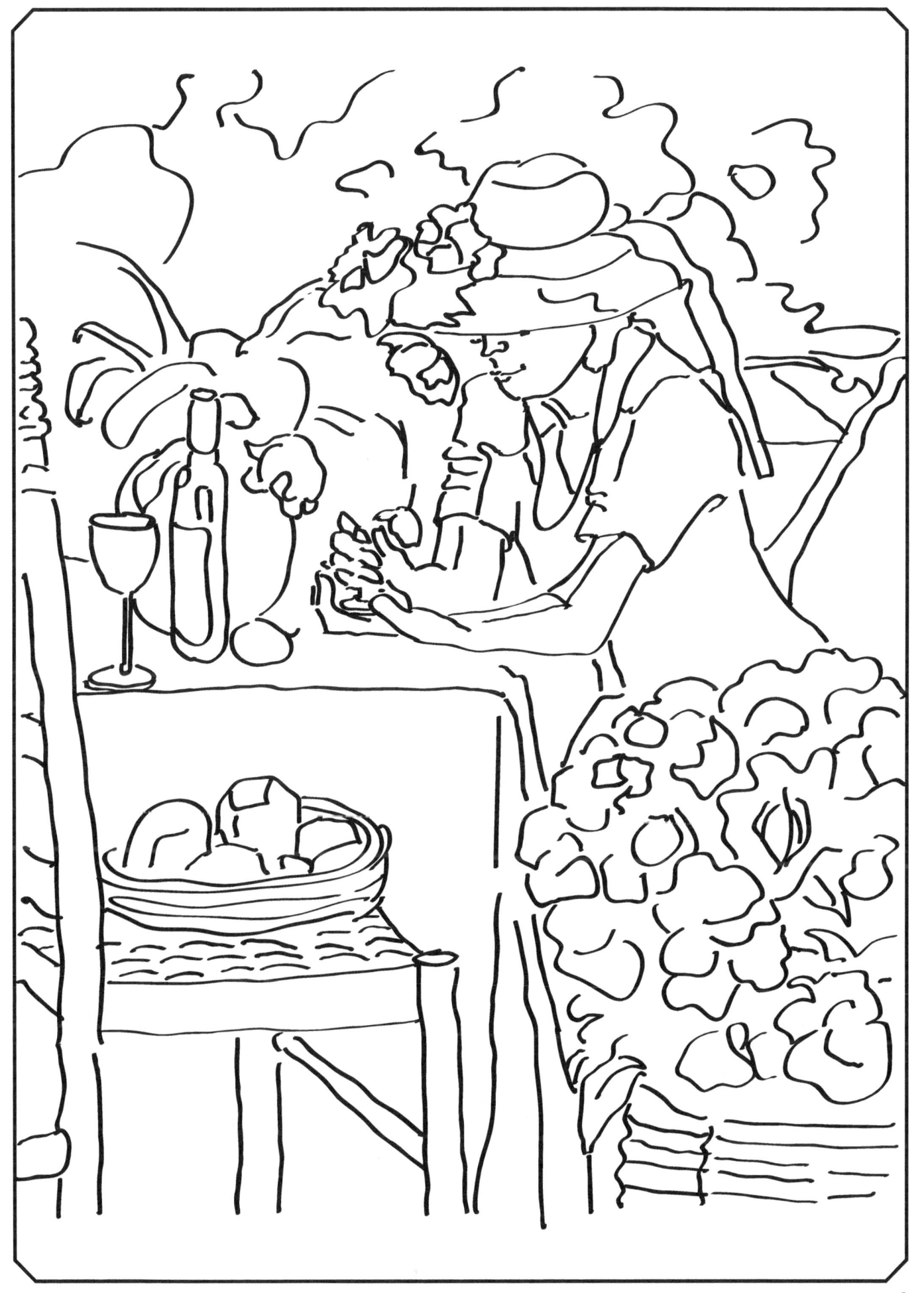

This Painting is called Summer Glow. You can even write in the label of your favorite wine. I believe it is a white wine due to the shape of the bottle.

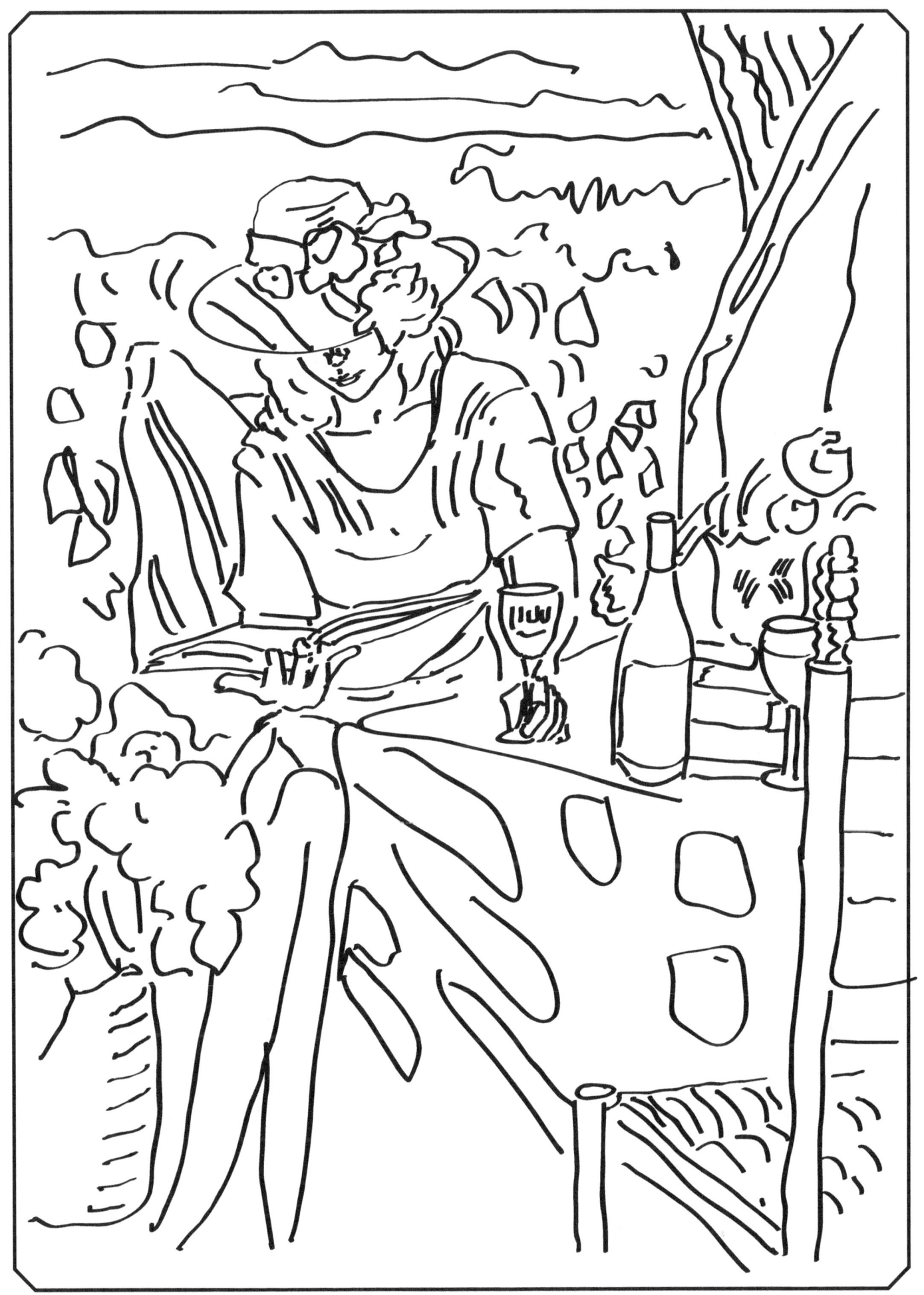

This painting is called The Lace Dress and is a very recent one. Again you have the big expanse of the tablecloth so change it up with some soft pastels and even try working white over the colors to blend them. The background here can be fun to mix light with dark.

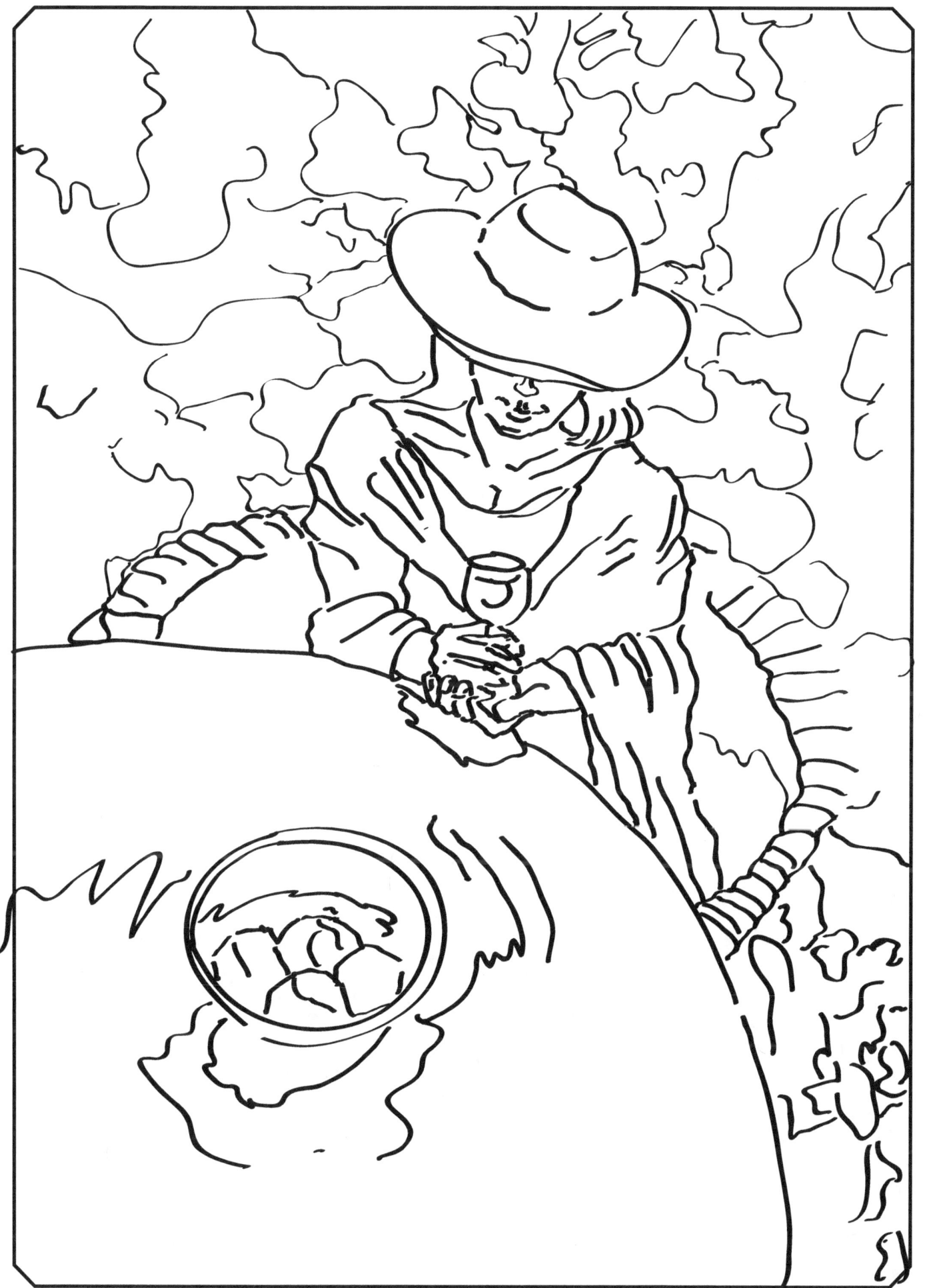

This painting is called Napa Retreat.

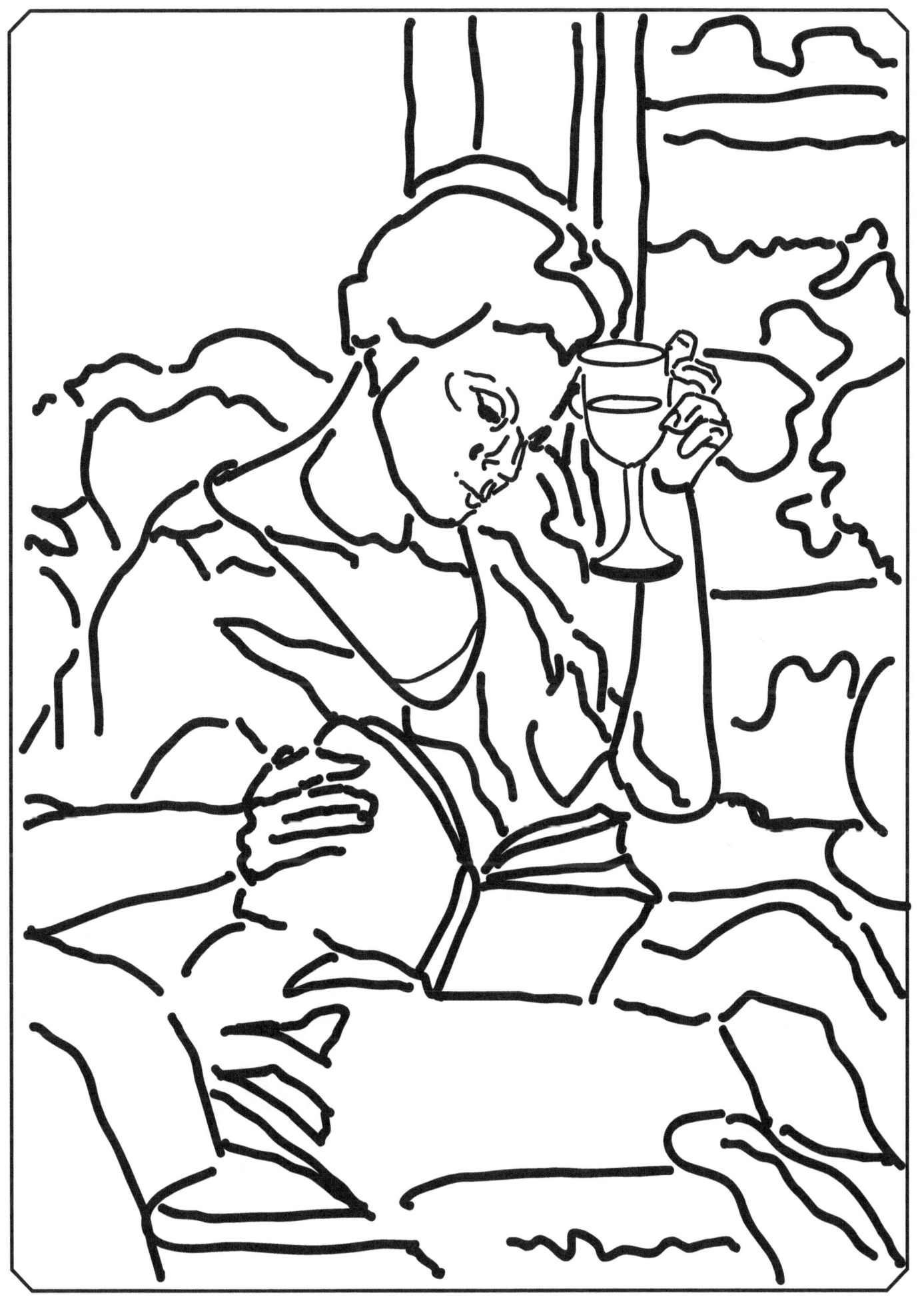

This painting is simply called Girl with Wine and maybe you could even write some words on the pages of the book if you use a very fine pen.

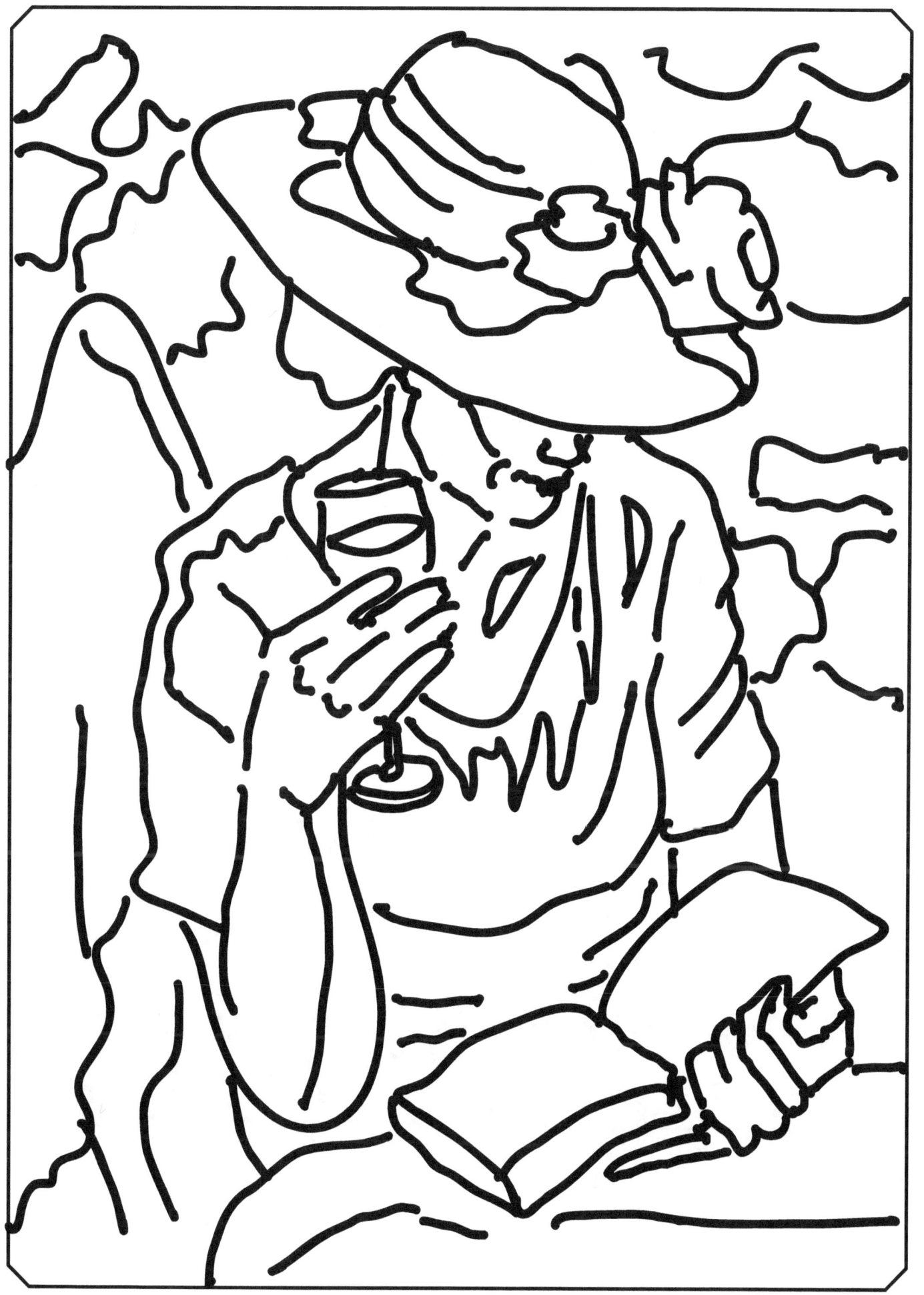

This painting is called Calla Lillies but it could also be called Cabernet because it is definitely a Cab bottle. Try prints, plaids, or stripes for the dress or a solid. It was in actuality a beautiful sky blue dress.

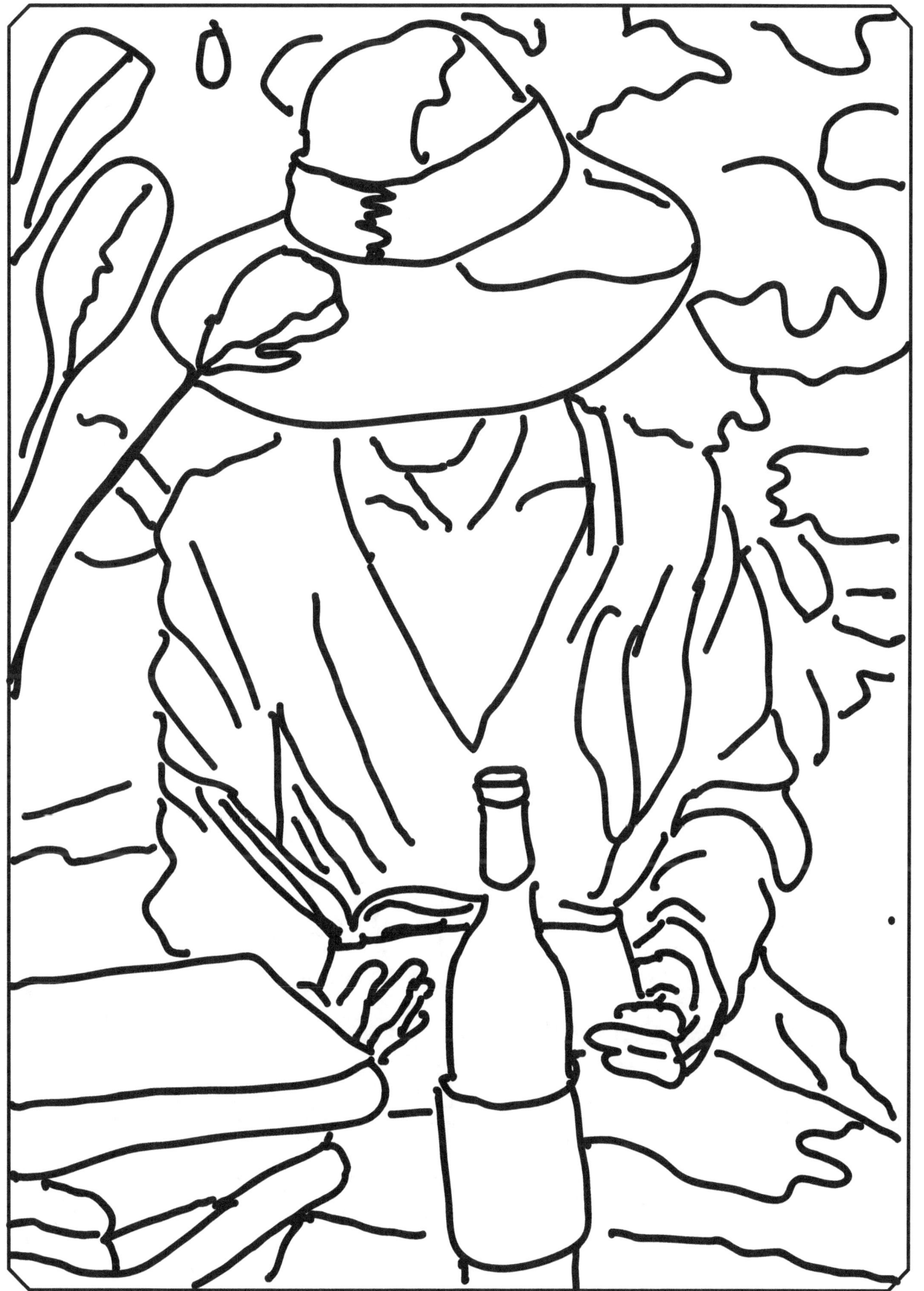

This painting is called Melancholy. Notice where the lines of shadow fall and try to be consistent.

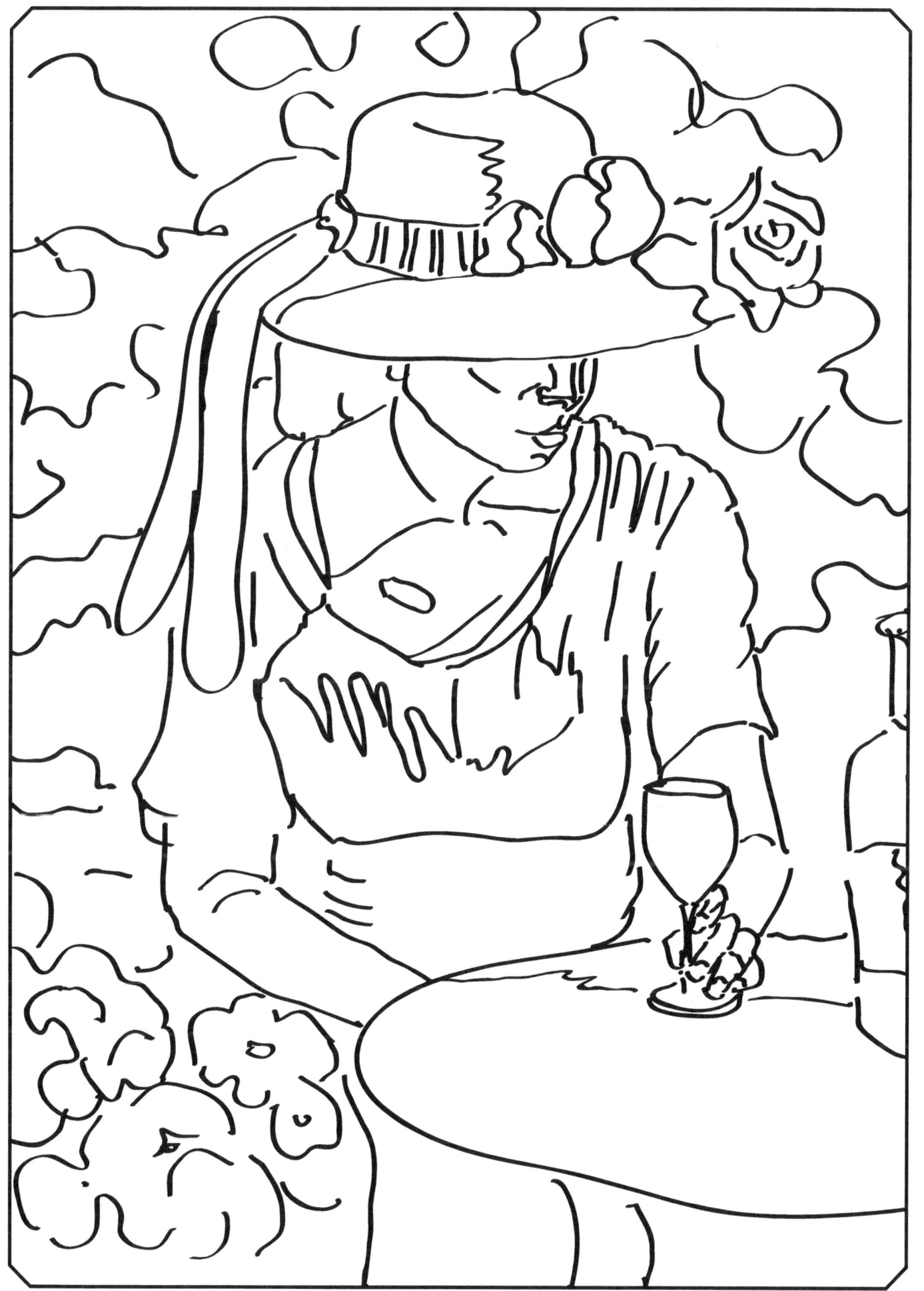

This Painting was etched onto a bottle of ZD Chardonnay for the Napa Valley Wine Auction. In the foreground is a hydrangea potted plant and the background is whatever you want it to be

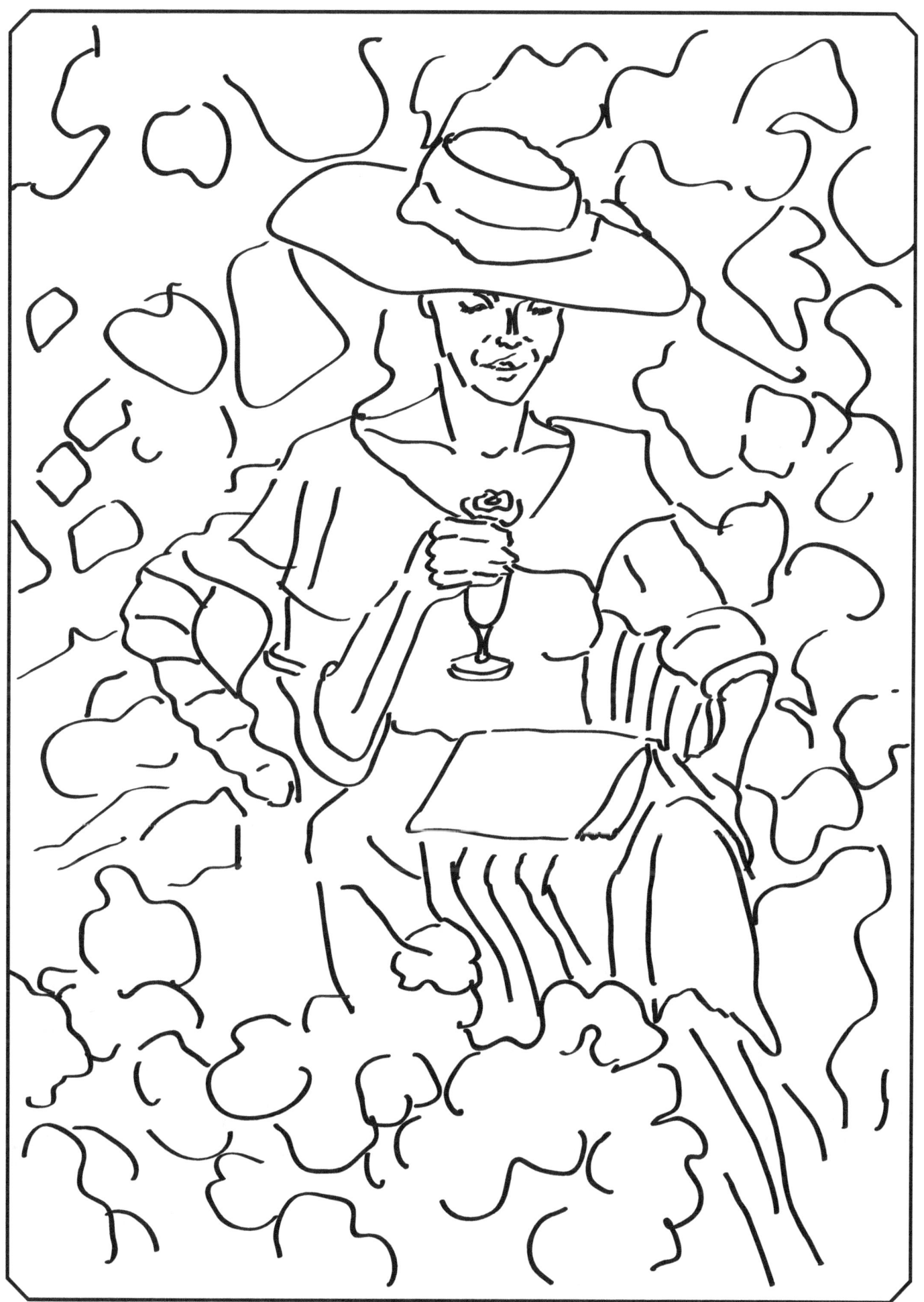

This painting is called Autumn Wine so it would be good in Autumn colors. You could invent a new name for the second version and make it Summer Wine.

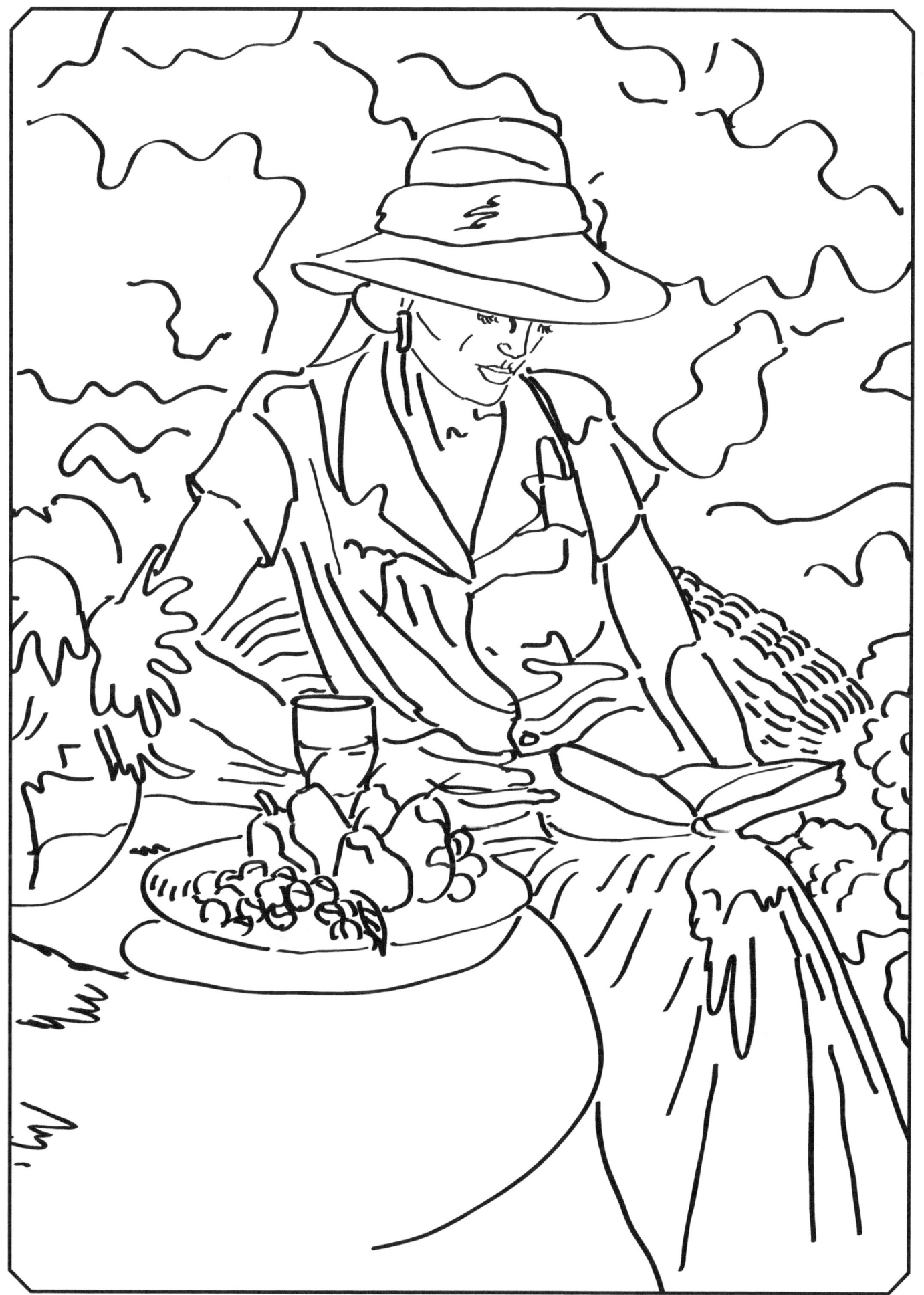

Notes

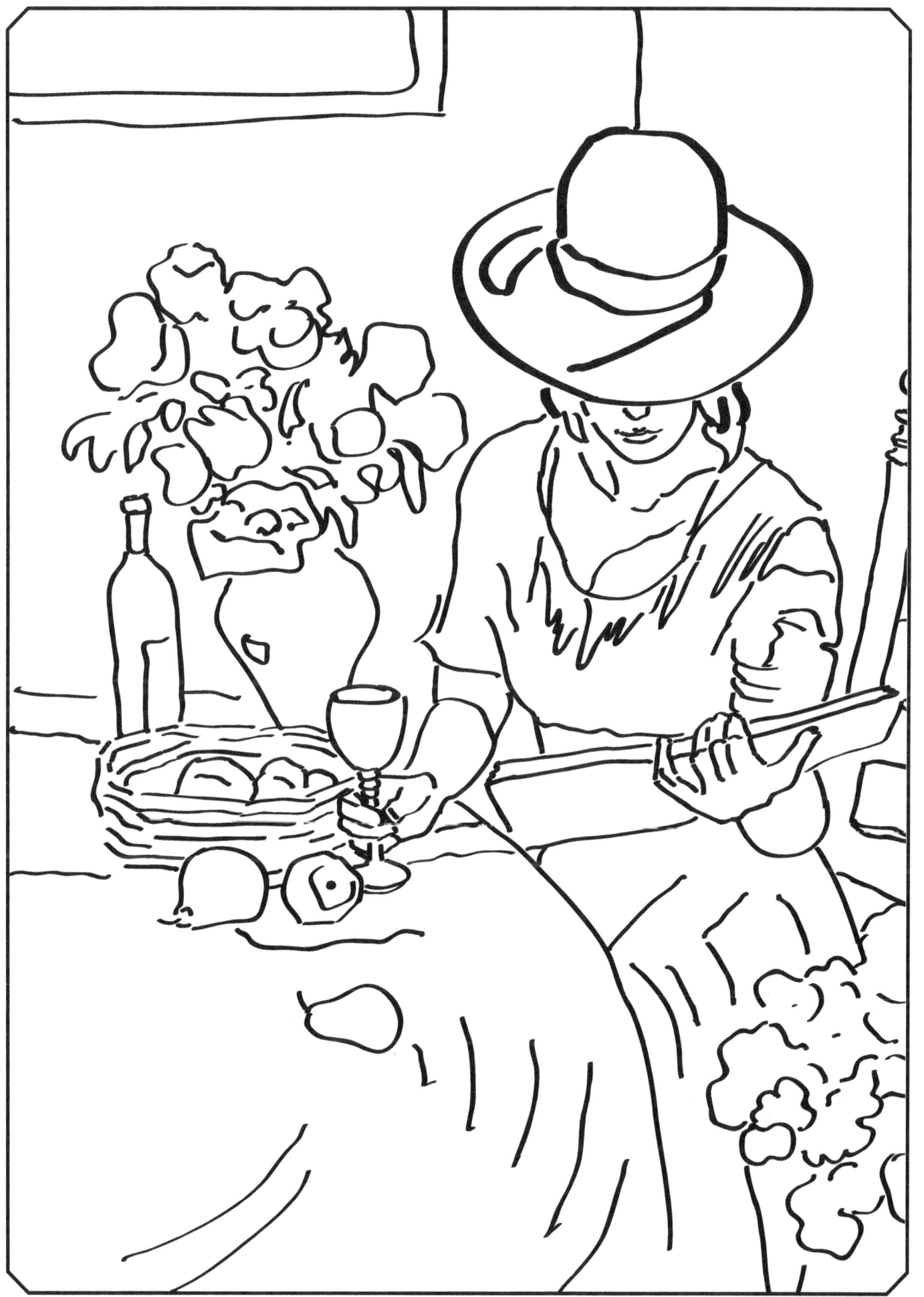

Notes

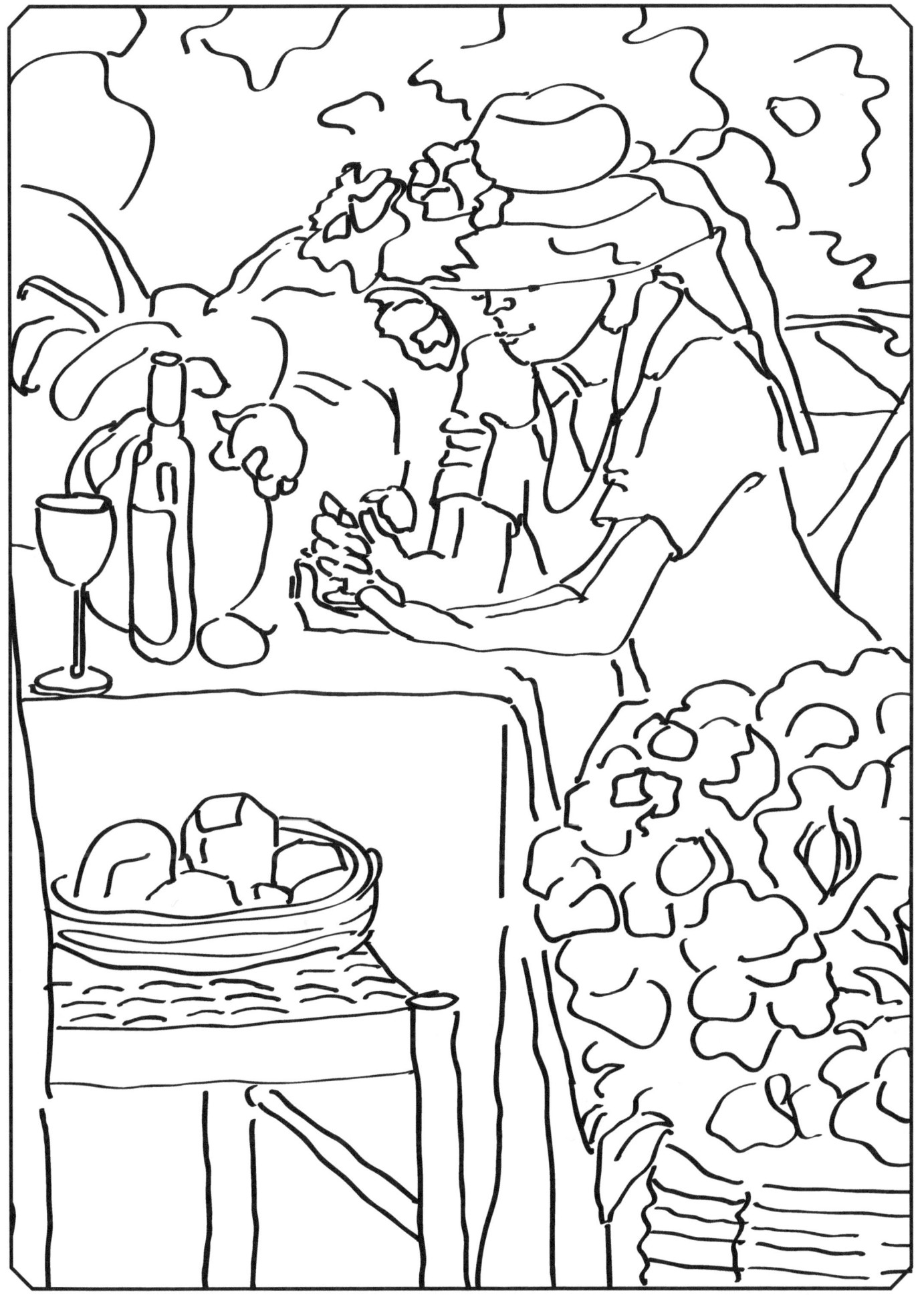

Notes

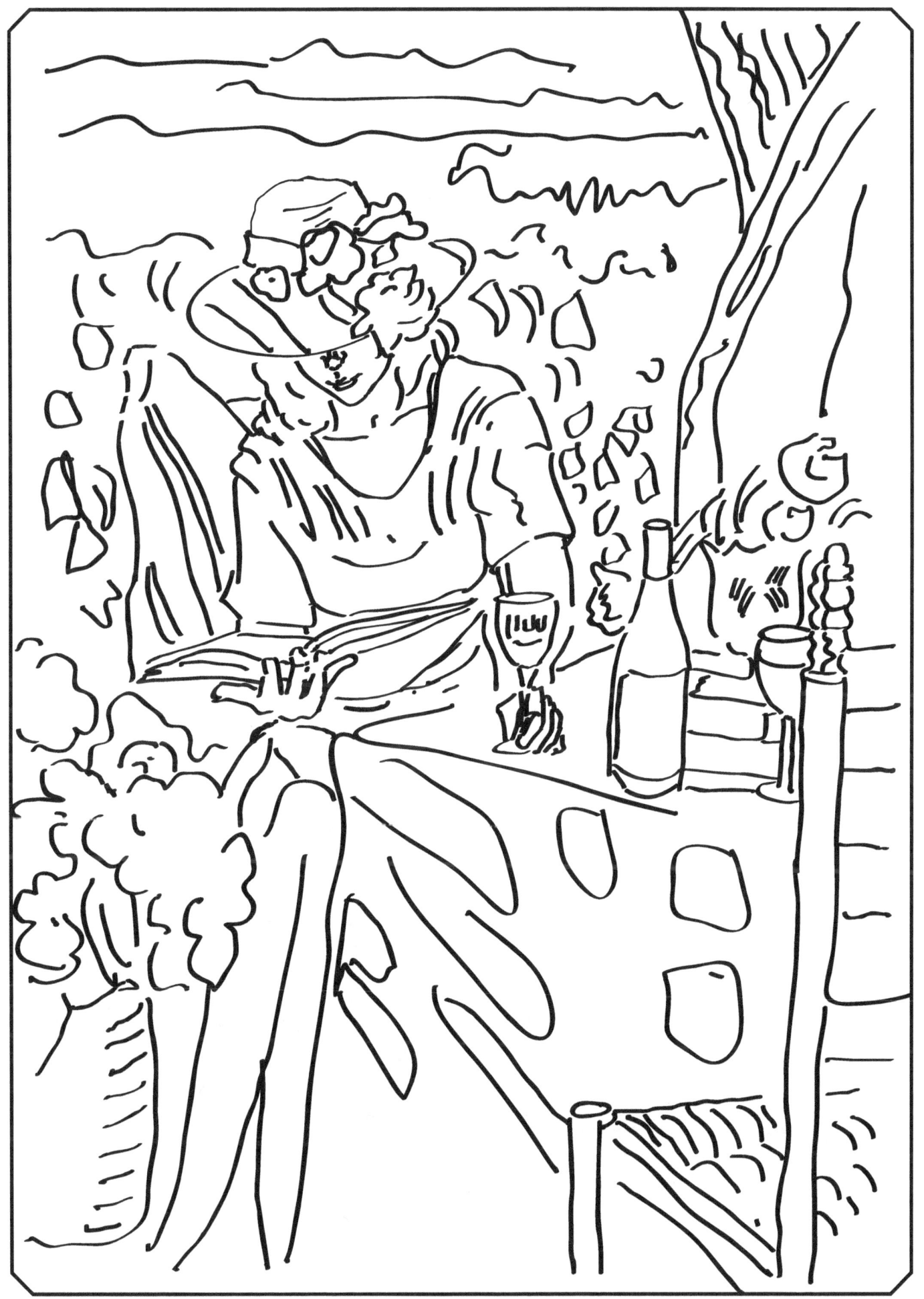

Notes

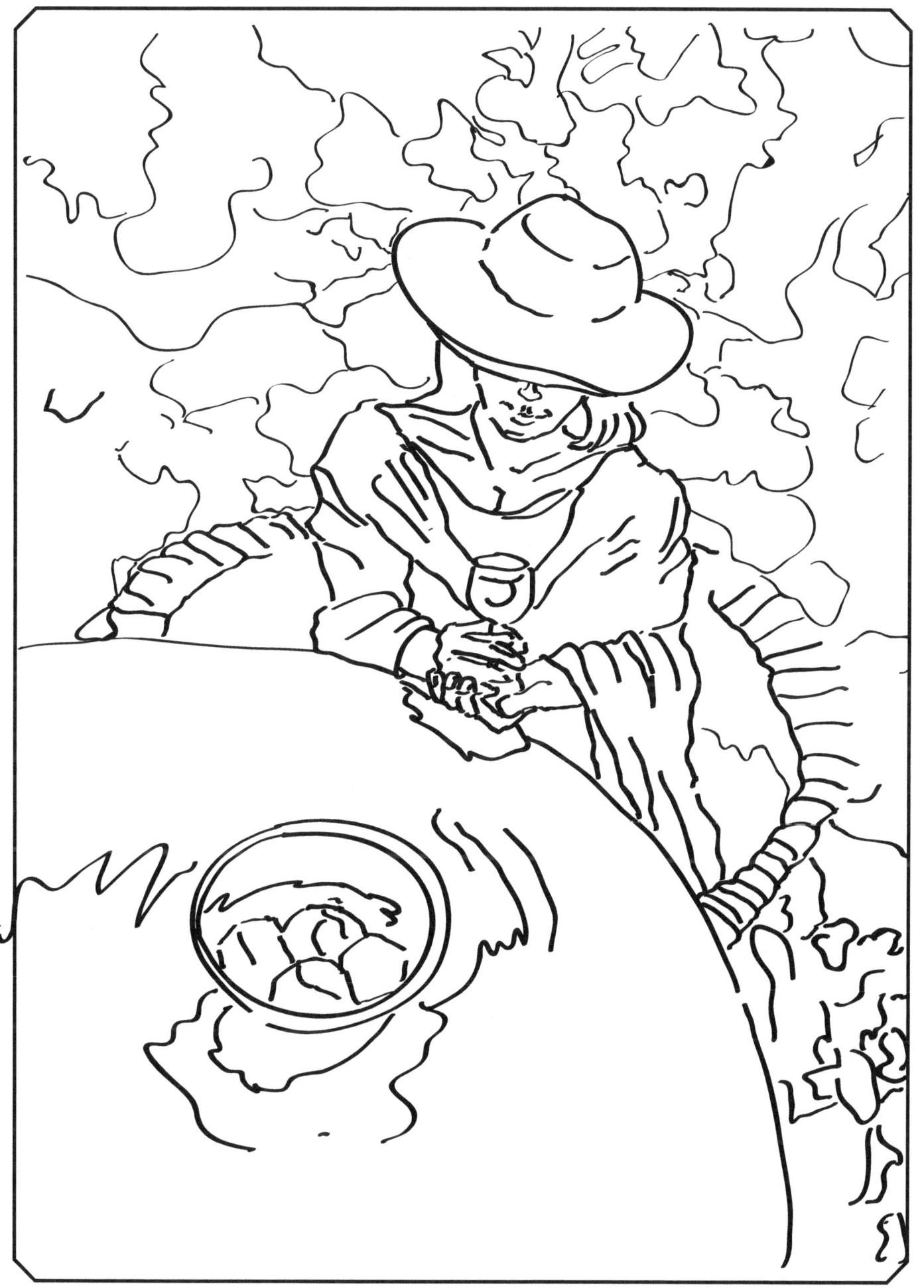

Notes

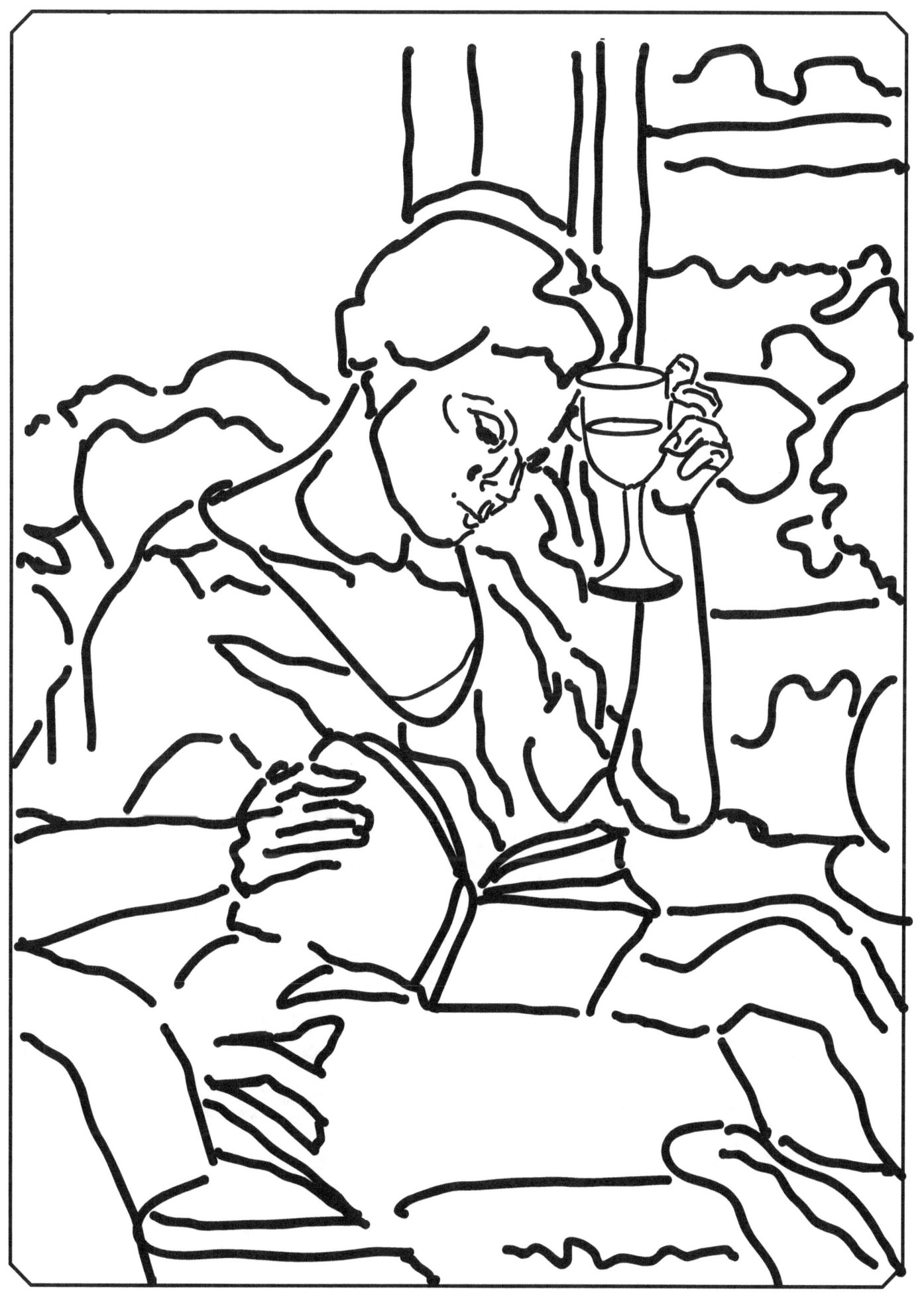

Notes

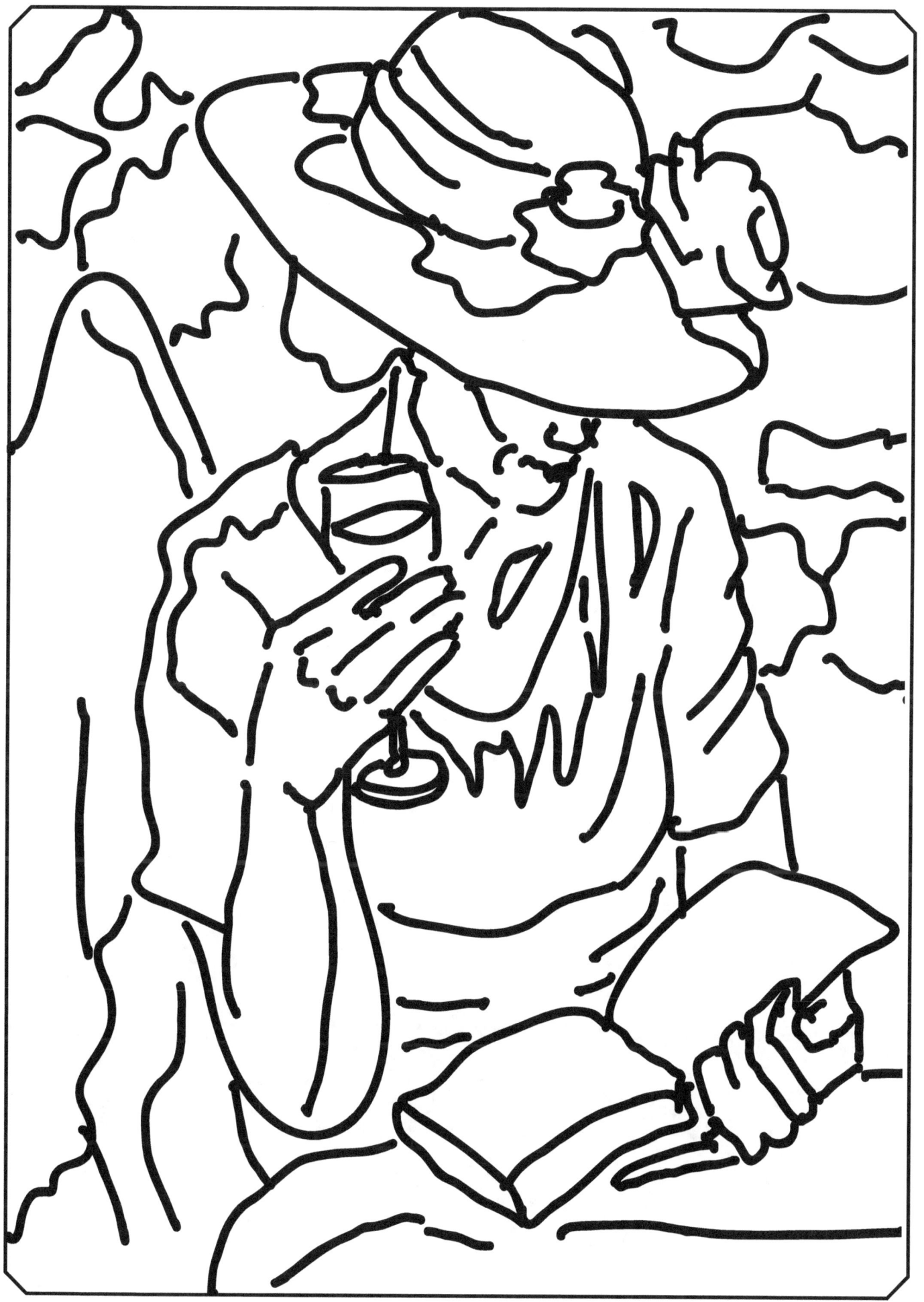

Notes

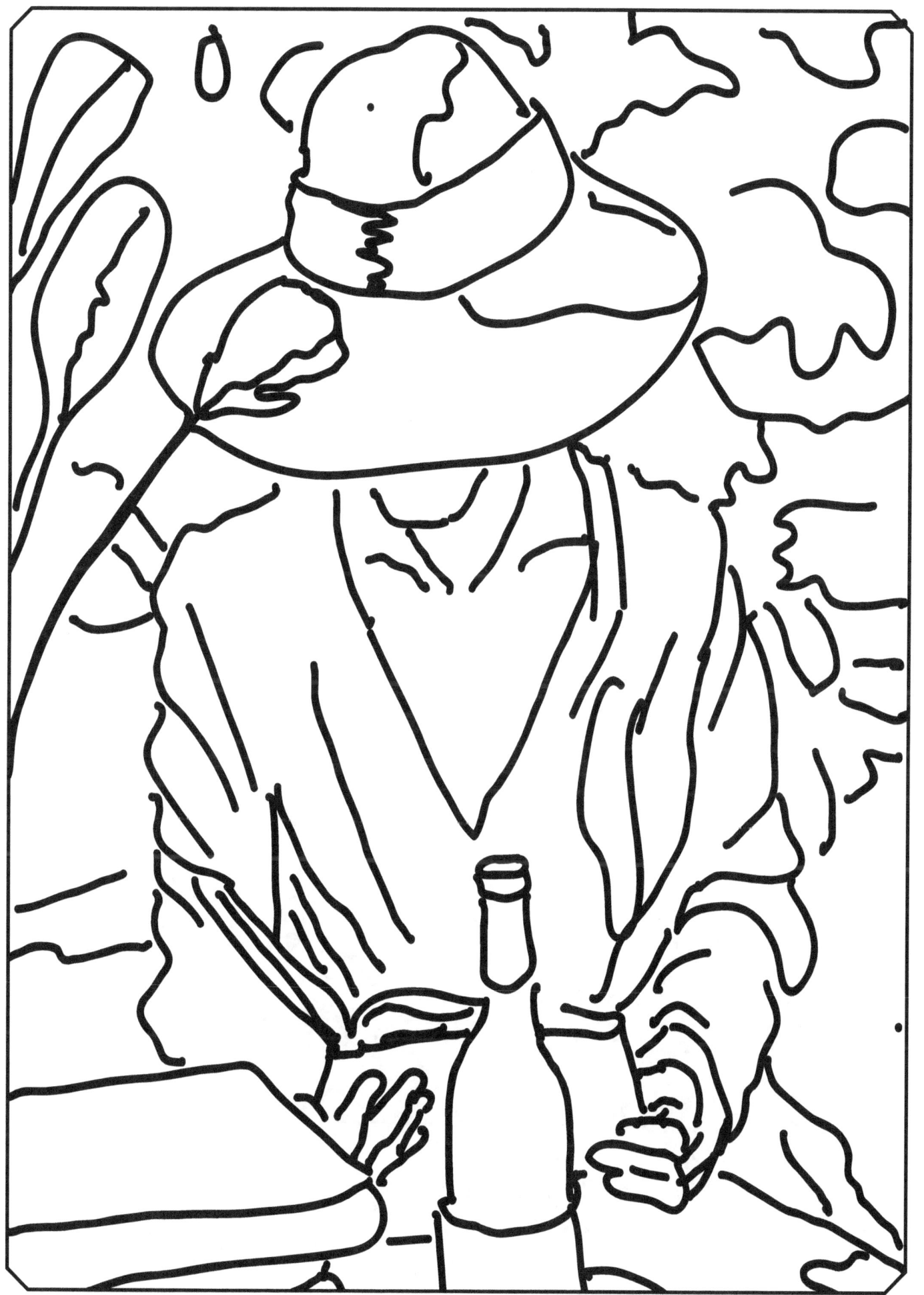

Notes

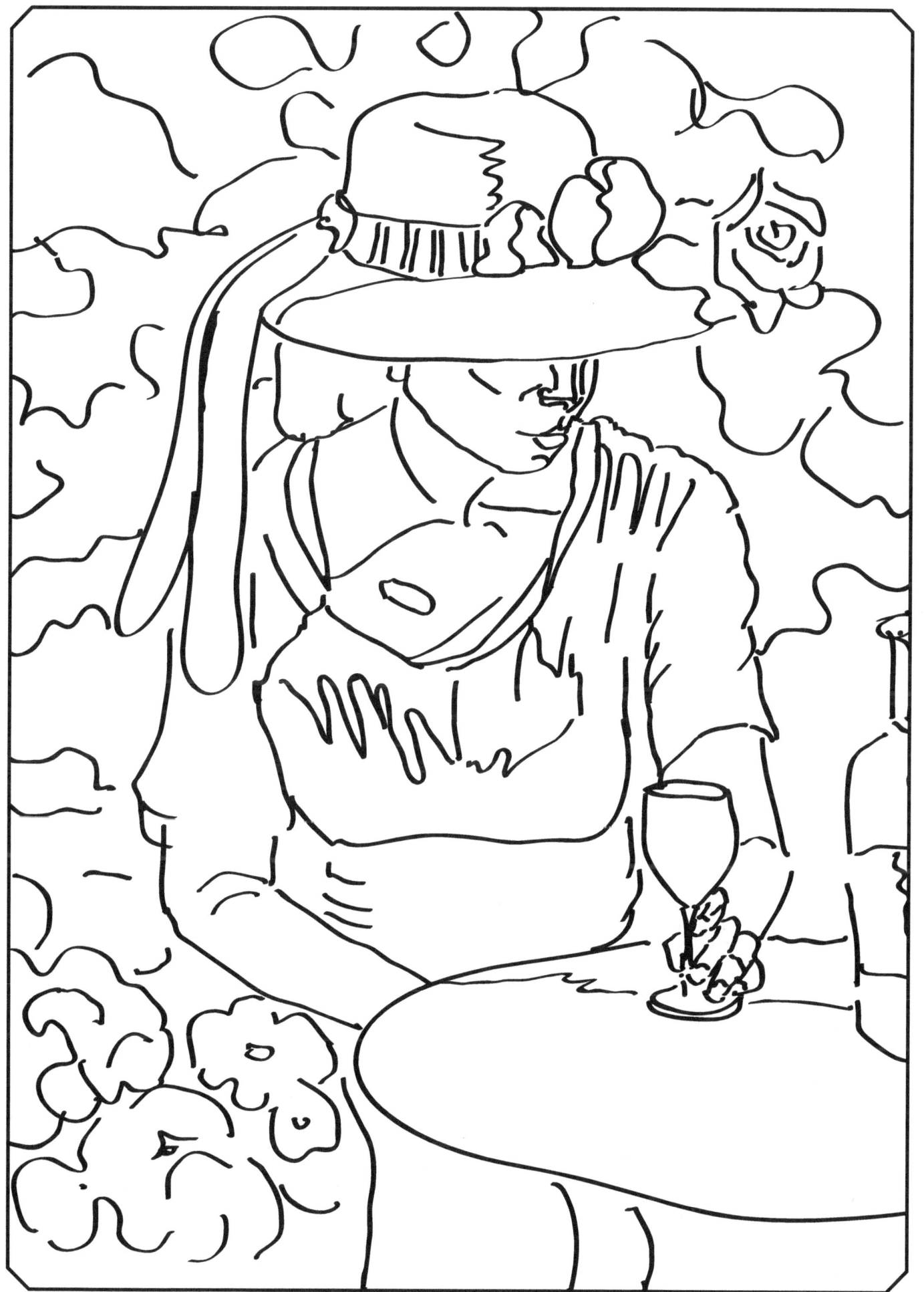

Notes

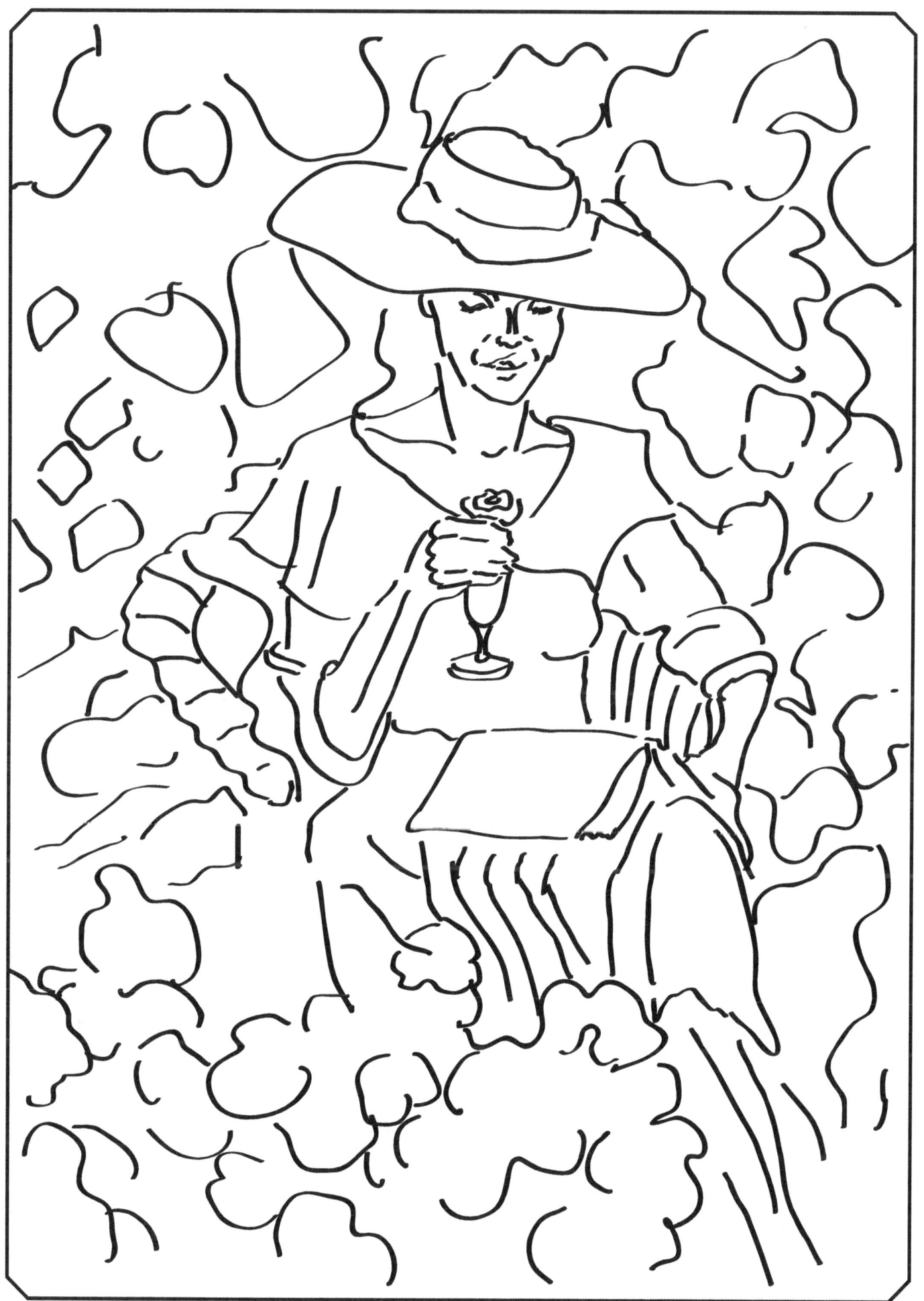

Notes

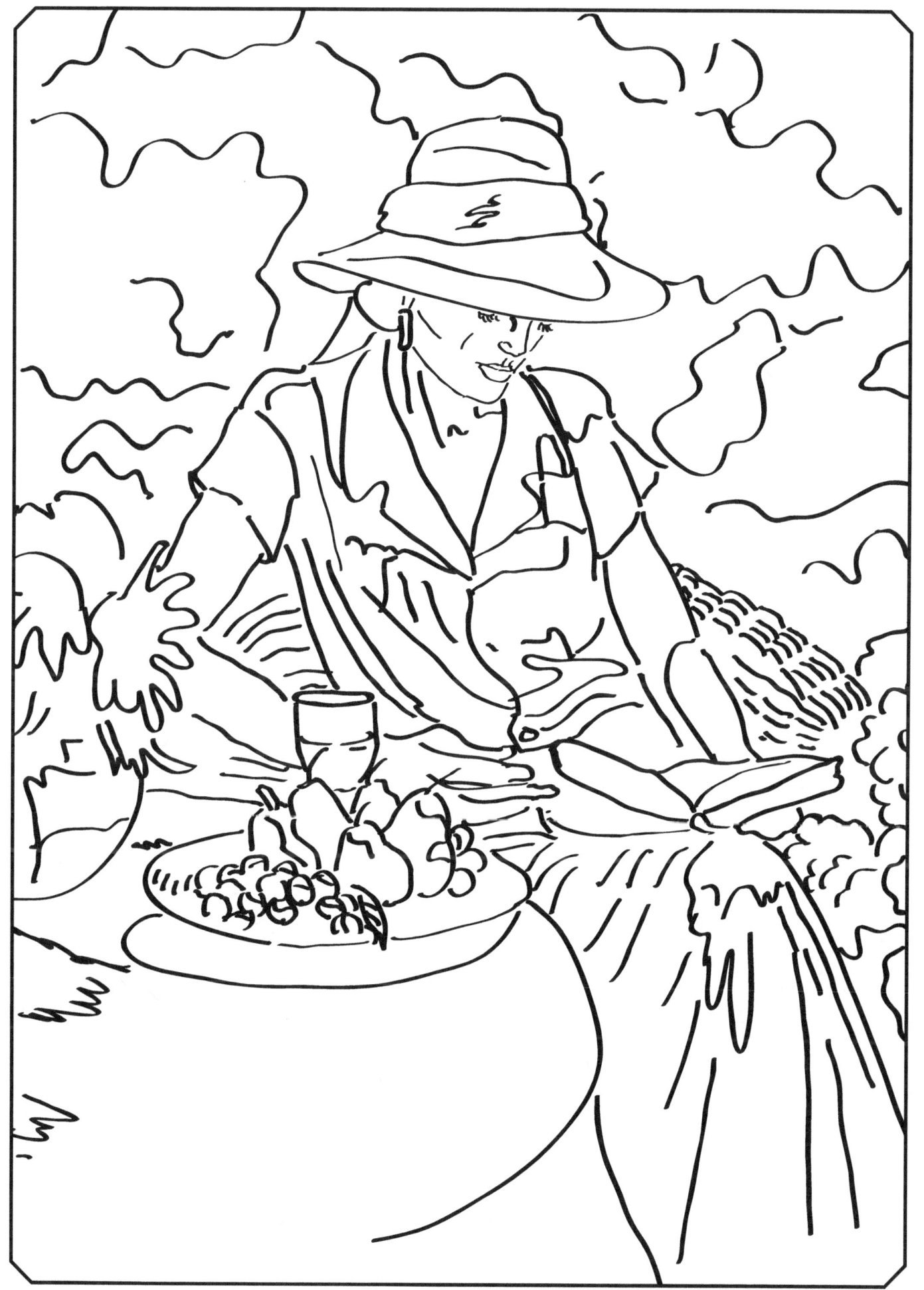

www.ingramcontent.com/pod-product-compliance
Lightning Source LLC
Chambersburg PA
CBHW081123240526
45470CB00019B/2931